credits

Library of Congress Cataloging-in-Publication Data

West, Donald.
Mountain Biking Northern Arkansas
Guide to the Ozarks and Arkansas River Valley

1. Mountain Biking
Arkansas Ozarks and Arkansas River Valley
Guide Books.

2. Arkansas Ozarks and Arkansas River Valley
Guide Books. I. Title.

Maps and photographs by Donald West
General design by Joal McCourt
Editing by Dave Wise

Layout, design, production and printing
Now Creative, Inc.
www.nowcreative.com
479-200-3761

Chainring Adventures
179 East 100 South
Alpine, Utah 84004

contents

from the
author

Welcome to Arkansas. If you have never ridden in Arkansas before, you're in for a real treat. Until now, Arkansas has gone without a definitive guide to singletrack trails open to mountain biking. This guide leads you to 21 of the best trails for mountain biking in the Arkansas Ozarks and Arkansas River Valley. Fifteen of the trails have never been published before. I have focused my efforts to share the locations of some of the best singletrack trails in the state. All of the trails in this book were mapped using a GPS for the most up-to-date information on trails. Mountain Biking Northern Arkansas is the most comprehensive guide to mountain bike trails in Arkansas.

Most of the trails in this guide are located within a short drive of several larger cities in the state, including: Fayetteville, Eureka Springs, Fort Smith, Mountain Home, Mountain View, Russelleville, and Little Rock. You'll be riding on land managed by private property owners and a variety of land management agencies, including Arkansas State Parks, United States Forest Service, U.S. Army Corps of Engineers, and Arkansas Game and Fish Commission. Make sure you review all the rules related to trail use before you venture out. The future of mountain bike trail access depends on your actions while visiting these areas, so make sure to ride responsibly and treat other trail users with respect.

The process of developing this trail guide has allowed me to explore some of the most beautiful corners of Arkansas. I spent countless hours mapping the trails throughout northern and central Arkansas, gathering information from topographic maps, talking to local bike shop employees, and asking friends in the mountain bike community about their favorite places to ride. I would like to thank Joal McCourt, Dave Renko and Eric Howerton for all their efforts in helping me make this book a reality.

I would also like to encourage all riders to get involved in the mountain bike community. Join a local club. Take a few hours out of your day to work on a trail. If you don't have a mountain bike club in your area, start one. The trail riding opportunities in your area will only improve with your efforts.

I hope you use this guide for many years to come, as you explore Arkansas. Keep your eyes open for a guide to Southern Arkansas in the near future. See you on the trail.

COMMON SENSE RULES

- Always wear a helmet
- Don't ride alone
- Take lots of water
- Bring a tool kit and first aid kit
- Yield to hikers and equestrians
- Treat water before drinking
- Read bulletin board at trailhead for current trail information
- Respect the rights of private landowners. Get permission before you go.

GEAR LIST

Here is a short list of the things you needed while on the trail
- Helmet
- Gloves
- Bike shoes
- Tire levers
- Spare tube and patch kit
- Allen wrenches (sizes appropriate for what you have on your bike)
- Pump with correct valve adaptor (presta/schrader)
- 6-inch crescent wrench
- Chain tool
- Spoke wrench
- Duct tape

USEFUL TOOLS

- Extra spokes
- Chain whip
- Cassette tool
- Needle nose pliers
- Full set of allen wrenches
- Brake pads
- Pedal wrench

FIRST AID KIT

- Suncreen
- Insect repellent
- Bandages
- Butterfly closure bandages
- Gauze pads (4"x4")
- Gauze roll
- Medical Tape
- Pain relievers and anti-itch medicine (Benadryl, aspirin, etc.)

How to use this guide

This book describes two geographic regions of Arkansas, including the Ozark Mountains and the Arkansas River Valley. Each trail description includes directions to the trailhead, difficulty rating, length, expected ride time, trail type, trail map, and contact information. There may also be special information about trail closures during certain times of year or information related to a private property owner, so please read the description completely before heading out.

Rating system

Trails are rated based upon their difficulty. Remember if you are not sure of your physical abilities, start with the easiest trails. Trail difficulty ratings are completely subjective. Riders should honestly assess their own physical abilities. Rides are described as easy, intermediate, and difficult, or a combination of two or more. The trail's rating is dependent on the ride length, its technical difficulty, and the amount of elevation change.

• Easy - most likely short, fairly smooth, and flat and demands little endurance and skills.
• Intermediate -long and technical enough to challenge any rider. Expect trails to have moderate elevation changes and include hazards such as roots, rocks, and creek crossings. Riders should possess intermediate riding skills and moderate physical endurance.
• Difficult - Demand greater riding skill, and the highest physical endurance. Difficult trails generally include large elevation changes, long distances, numerous trail hazards including exposure, exposed roots and rocks, and tight twisting trail layout, and require riders to be completely self sufficient.

Weather in Arkansas

Spring is one of the best times to ride in the Ozarks. Temperatures are mild ranging from the 60-80's during the day and drop into the 40-50's at night. Early in the spring the trees still don't have leaves, so there are some great views. The dogwood trees are in bloom, and there are numerous wildflowers. This is usually the time of year that it rains, so avoid riding on trails that stay wet. This can lead to increased soil erosion and maintenance costs for the trail. Check with local bike shops to get the latest information on trail conditions.

Summer in Arkansas can be hot and humid. Temperatures range from the 80-90's during the day with matching humidity levels. Temperatures in the 100's are not uncommon in July and August. Low temperatures range from the 60-70's. Summer thunderstorms can lower temperatures occasionally. Watch out for ticks, chiggers, and poison ivy, which can be prolific along the trail. I recommend riding early in the morning or late in the afternoon to avoid the heat of the day. Don't forget to break out the bike light for a few night rides. Make sure to bring plenty of water and insect repellent.

Fall is by far the best time of year to ride in the Ozarks. The Ozarks are full of hardwood trees, and that makes for a colorful fall. Mountainsides and valleys are splashed with yellows, reds, and oranges that nearly overwhelm the senses when colors are at their peak. Temperatures are very similar to spring, with temperature in the 60-80's during the day and the 30-50's at night. You can expect some rain this time of year as well. It's not unusual to have a storm stick around for a few days of constant light rain. It's also important to be aware of hunting seasons when riding, especially when venturing out on public land. During these times, wear an orange vest and avoid riding early in the morning and late in the evening when hunters are more likely to be in the woods. Remember, it is illegal to interfere with legal hunting in Arkansas.

With the leaves out of the way, winter can be the best time to be out in the woods in Arkansas. Stop and enjoy the scenery while the leaves are off. Remember that most of the trails will be covered in leaves that hide rocks and other obstacles on the trail. Temperatures can get cold at times, but if you dress in layers, you should be able to ride throughout the winter. Expect highs in the 40-50's and the lows in the teens and 20's. It's not uncommon for the temperature to drop below zero. Be prepared for snow, freezing rain, and sleet any time between November and March.

Rules of the trail

In certain areas of the country, mountain biking has become an unpopular activity with some land managers due to the actions of a few irresponsible trail users. If mountain bikers are to maintain access to trails in Arkansas, we must follow the International Mountain Bike Association (IMBA) Rules of the Trail. Don't forget that your actions speak louder than words.

International Mountain Bike Association (IMBA) rules of the trail

Ride on Open Trails. Respect the trail rules and laws. Riding on closed trails makes mountain bikers look bad. If you want to do something about a closed trail, contact your local mountain bike club and help out. If there is no club in your area, start one. For more information about how to start a mountain bike club, contact the International Mountain Bike Association (IMBA) at 303-545-9011.

Leave No Trace. Practice low-impact cycling and pack out all trash. While you're at it, pick up someone else's trash too. Please stay on the trail at all times and do not take shortcuts.

Control Your Bicycle. If you can't control your bike, you might hurt yourself. Or worse, you could hurt somebody else. Remember a little courtesy goes a long way. Don't skid around corners or ride on wet trails. These activities can increase soil erosion, turning your favorite trail into an unrideable mess.

Don't Scare Animals. You should avoid scaring horses, livestock, and wildlife whenever possible. An unannounced approach, a sudden movement, or a loud noise startles animals. This can be dangerous for you, horse riders, and those around you. Give animals extra room and time to adjust to you. Always leave gates the way you found them when riding on private or public land.

Plan Ahead. Let other people know where you are going and how long you plan to be gone. Make sure you have the proper clothes for the weather conditions. A well-planned trip is self-satisfying and less of a burden on others.

the ozarks

The Ozark-St. Francis National Forest covers over 1.2 million acres of land mostly in the Boston Mountains and Ozark Plateau in Northern Arkansas. Smaller sections of the forest are located just south of the Arkansas River and in eastern Arkansas. Mt. Magazine, the highest point in Arkansas at 2,753 feet, is located just south of the Arkansas River near Paris, Arkansas. Blanchard Springs Caverns, one of Arkansas's underground treasures, is located near Mountain View, Arkansas. The National Forest offers a wide variety of recreational opportunities including mountain biking, boating, canoeing, fishing, swimming, camping, horseback riding, ATV use, driving, and wildlife watching. There are five wilderness areas to explore. Six nationally recognized wild and scenic rivers course through the landscape including the Buffalo National River, Mulberry River, Big Piney, Sylamore Creek, Richland Creek, and the Illinois Bayou. Strap on a pair of hiking boots and take on the 165-mile Ozark Highlands trail, the 51-mile Buffalo River Trail, or any other of the hundreds of miles of hiking trails that pierce into the Arkansas backcountry. Catch some smallmouth and largemouth bass on Crooked Creek, Kings River, or Sylamore creek. Try out your luck catching record rainbow, cutthroat, and brown trout on the tailwaters of Beaver Lake, Bull Shoals, Norfork, or Greer's Ferry Lake. If you love rock climbing, head to Byrd's Adventure Center along the Mulberry River, Horseshoe Canyon near Jasper, and Sam's Throne near Mount Judea. Try your luck hunting deer, black bear, and wild turkey. If you love to drive, check out scenic Highway 71 between Fayetteville and Alma, Highway 23 "the Pig Trail" between Fayetteville and Ozark, or Highway 7 between Harrison and Russelleville. You can spend a lifetime exploring the wonders of Ozark National Forest. For more information, turn to the reference section in the back of the book.

Trail Advocacy

Mountain biking is a wonderful activity that deserves your support. You can ensure the future of this sport by joining a local mountain bike club. There are several local mountain bike clubs in Arkansas and national organizations that are working on keeping our trails open. Get involved by letting land managers know that mountain bikers are a legitimate trail user group who deserve to have places to ride. Mountain bike clubs organize trail maintenance trips, work with land managers on private and public land, and lead organized group rides. These clubs can always use your support. Make it a point to volunteer your time or your funds on a trail project near you. As more people get involved in advocacy, trail opportunities will improve. For more information about mountain bike clubs in Arkansas, turn to the reference section in the back of the book.

GENERAL TRAIL LOCATION MAP

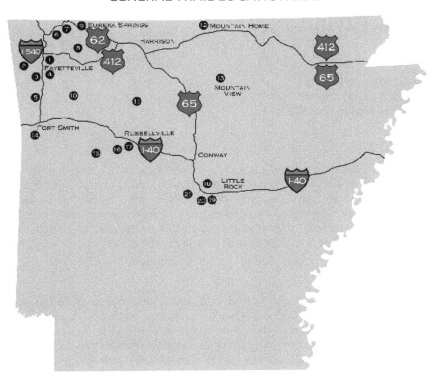

Ozark Mountains
1. Lake Fayetteville Trail
2. Twin Knobs Trail
3. Dennis Moore Trail
4. Lake Wilson Trail
5. Devil's Den State Park Trails
6. Hobbs State Park—Conservation Area
7. Lost Bridge Village—North
8. Madison County WMA
9. Lake Leatherwood Trail System
10. Mill Creek Trail System
11. Mocassin Gap Trail System
12. Pigeon Creek Trail System
13. Syllamo Trail System

Arkansas River Valley
14. Springhill Park Trail
15. Huckleberry Mtn. Trail System
16. Mount Nebo Trail
17. Old Post Trail
18. Camp Robinson Trail System
19. Allsopp Park Trail
20. Boyle Park Trail
21. Section 13 Trail

Lake Fayetteville Trail
Easy

Trail length: 5 miles
Ride time: 35-45 minutes
Trail type: Mostly singletrack

directions

This trail is located on the north side of Fayetteville near the Northwest Arkansas Mall on College Ave. You can park at the trailhead on the north side of the lake by turning right on Lake Fayetteville Rd., then follow the road past the baseball fields and through the gates. The parking area is at the end of the road. Veteran's Park is on the south side of the lake. From College Ave., turn east on Zion Rd. The park entrance will be on the left shortly after passing the Lowes store.

trail description

Lake Fayetteville Trail is one of the most popular trails in northwest Arkansas, due to easy access and the fact that it is beginner friendly. Trailheads are located on the north and south side of the lake. Starting at the north trailhead, you will climb up a short incline, then turn right and follow a road for a while. After crossing the road to the environmental science center, turn left and climb up the hill. After topping the hill, descend to a bridge for the first of three creek crossings. You can thank the Boy Scouts for the bridges on this trail. The trail swings through the trees and breaks out into a large meadow. Follow the edge of the property around the meadow, then descend into a small ravine and out again. You'll gradually descend some more, passing over another bridge and then crossing the largest bridge on the trail over Clear Creek. Climb up again for a little while before dropping down again to another field. Follow the edge of the woods and cross another small creek. This area is located next to the Fayetteville Botanical Gardens, which are a must see if you have the time. The trail now dives into the woods again for the best part of the trail. You'll snake in and out of several ravines before coming out at Veteran's Park. Continue on the road and stay to the right. Before the road turns to the left to leave the park, the trail starts again on the right. You'll cross a new bridge spanning the spillway. Cross the dam and turn

There are restrooms available at Veteran's Park. Other amenities include a sand volleyball court, playground, and a pavilion. There is a Frisbee golf course on the north side of the lake. You can try your hand fishing on the lake or enjoy an afternoon in a kayak for a minimal fee. Stop by the marina or call Steve Hatfield for current costs. The Lake Fayetteville Trail is closed after dark. For more information contact Steve Hatfield, City Parks and Recreation Director, at 479-444-3471, Ext. 688.

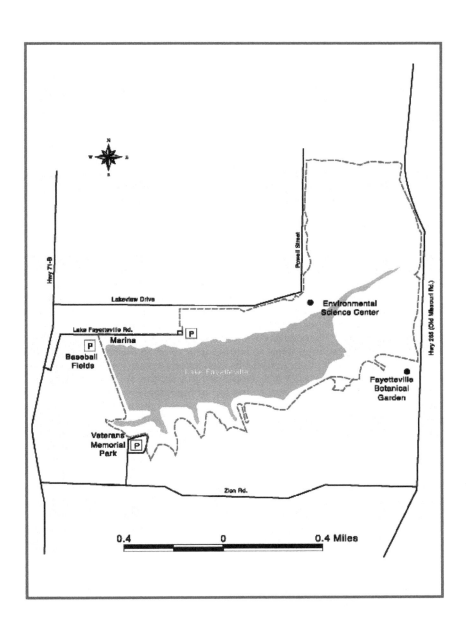

Twin Knobs Trail

Intermediate

Trail length: 7.5 miles – one way
Ride time: 1 ½ hour-2 hours
Trail type: singletrack and short sections of doubletrack

directions

This trail is located west of Fayetteville. Drive 13 miles west on Highway 16 to Lake Wedington. From Siloam Springs, take Highway 16 east 12 miles to Lake Wedington. The trailhead is on the north side of the road across from the lake.

trail description

The Twin Knobs Trail has just recently opened to mountain bikers thanks to the advocacy efforts of the Ozark Off Road Cyclists. From the trailhead you'll climb quickly to the top of the first hill and drop into and out of several hollows before coming to an old roadbed. Turn right on the road. You'll pass to the right of a spring that spills into an intermittent stream. Follow the road for a short distance, then make a sharp left back on to singletrack. This section of trail is a blast as it twists and turns through a pine grove. The needles cover the forest floor making the trail completely smooth. You'll need to drop down to a lower gear to make the sharp climb to the first road crossing. The trail crosses WC 849, then follows a bluff line. This is one of the most scenic parts of the trail. You'll climb through a section of the bluff that broke off the main bluff line on the way to the top of the ridge. Before you head down the other side of the ridge, check out the great views to the west. The trail crosses the road again before descending into the next valley. Take some time to enjoy the wide variety of wildflowers, if you are riding in the spring. You'll follow the valley for nearly a mile before climbing a steep, long, narrow ridge and crossing another Forest Service access road. You'll follow the base of the first knob on the east (this section can be very muddy after a rain) and cross a flat ridge before coming to your first trail intersection. Drop down to the right to take a quick dip in the Illinois River. It's a great place to cool down when the temperatures rise. If you continue forward, you will climb gradually at first then climb steeply up to the top of the second mountain. There is a great view back to the south when the leaves are off the trees. Head back the same way you came or utilize the Forest Service roads shown on the map to get

Lake Wedington has campsites available for tents and RVs or treat yourself to one of the C.C.C. era log cabins. Lake Wedington offers a swimming area, picnic tables, sand volleyball courts, and canoe rentals. The hiking trail around the lake is off limits to mountain bikes. The Twin Knobs Trail is closed to horses and off-road vehicles. Please notify a national forest park ranger if you see illegal use. You can find out more about the area by contacting the U.S. Forest Service office in Ozark, AR, at 479-667-2191. There is also information available at www.fs.fed.us/oonf/ozark.

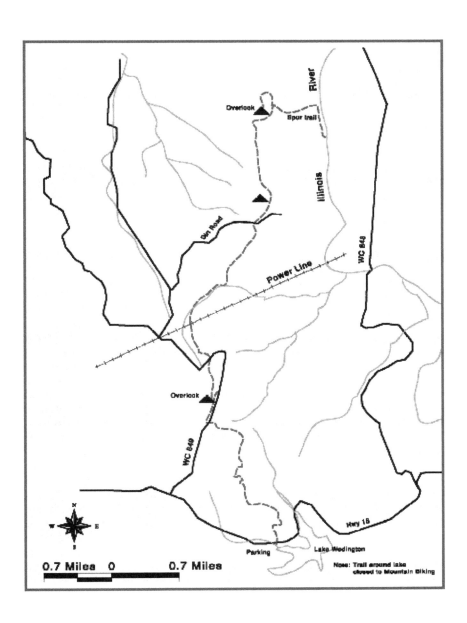

Overlook

Spur trail

River

Illinois

Dim Road

Power Line

WC 848

Overlook

WC 848

Hwy 16

Parking

Lake Wedington

Note: Trail around lake closed to Mountain Biking

N
W   E
S

0.7 Miles   0   0.7 Miles

Dennis Moore Trail

Difficult

Trail length: 5.5 miles
Ride time: 45 minutes – 1 hour
Trail type: singletrack

directions

This trail is located near Farmington, Arkansas. From the intersection of Interstate 540 and Hwy. 62 in Fayetteville. Head west on Hwy. 62 to Farmington. Turn left on Hwy. 170. Follow this road 4.75 miles, then turn left on Washington County 254 (dirt road). Drive 0.4 miles to a private drive (straight at second 90 degree turn) to the trailhead. Park on the right side of the road. You'll know you're at the right place if you see a water tower on the hill above you.

trail description

Dennis Moore has graciously allowed mountain bikers and hikers on his property for years, so please show respect when riding on his property. Dennis built a very challenging trail, so make sure you assess your abilities before attempting this ride. From the trailhead, head straight up the gravel road to the water tower. Dennis has built some gates that allow hikers and mountain bikers to pass through while leaving the gates shut. Please leave the gates the way you found them. From the water tower, follow the trail to the right along the contour of the mountain. You'll reach an old road bed that climbs steeply to the top of the mountain. Once on top, there are some great views of the surrounding country. Follow the trail to the right and skirt around the ridge, before dropping off the other side for a hair-raising descent. The trail levels off before you make a steep climb back to the ridge. Be prepared to drop down to the granny gear to make it up this steep pitch. Once back on top, you'll twist and turn back and forth across the hilltop. There is a really cool bridge that spans a gap in a bluff. Drop down on the front side of the mountain again and then turn right straight down the hill crossing the entrance trail. Watch out for a sweeping turn to the right, then back to the left through some technical rock gardens. Follow the trail gradually uphill again along a challenging bench before turning sharply to the right. Next, you drop steeply through a bluff line to a pasture. Keep to the left and continue to descend through a short section of woods to another pasture. Follow the fence line then follow the trail up to the right. Turn sharply to the left and enter your last section of rocky trail through the woods. You'll pop out close to the road you climbed up earlier. Head uphill for another lap or turn left and head back to your vehicle.

Please contact Dennis Moore at 479-267-6140 before riding on the trail. Otherwise, meet up with a local club ride out of the bike shops in Fayetteville. There is no restroom or water on site, so bring everything you need. Dennis has requested that mountain bikers stay off the trails when they are wet. Remember it is a privilege, not a right, to ride on these trails.

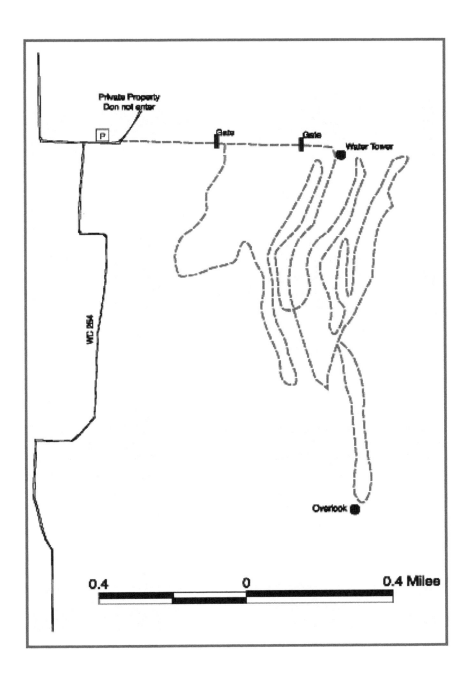

Private Property
Do not enter

P

Gate

Gate

Water Tower

WC 264

Overlook

0.4   0   0.4 Miles

Lake Wilson Trail

Intermediate

4

Trail length: 2.5 miles
Ride time: 30-40 minutes
Trail type: singletrack

directions

This trail is located on the south side of Fayetteville, AR, near Drake Field Airport. From the intersection of Hwy. 71 and Hwy. 156, drive 1.5 miles east on Hwy. 156 to Wilson Hollow Road. Turn right on Wilson Hollow Road and drive 1.5 miles to a T-intersection. Turn left and continue on Wilson Hollow Road to Lake Wilson Park. The trailhead is approximately 0.75 miles from the T-intersection. There will be a small pavilion next to the parking area.

trail description

Lake Wilson Trail is fairly short, but it packs in a lot of scenery in 2.5 miles of trail. If you are interested in making this a longer ride, you can start in town or begin at the intersection of Hwy. 156 and Wilson Hollow Road. From the trailhead, follow the edge of the lake for a while. There is a steep creek crossing about halfway into the trail that requires most riders to dismount. Then you'll cross another small stream that flows into Lake Wilson. Follow the trail to the first trail intersection. The best way to ride the loop is to turn right at the intersection, but the loop is fun in both directions. If you follow the trail to the right, you will climb steeply uphill for a while. You'll weave through some large, moss-covered boulders before climbing steeply to an old roadbed. Turn left on the roadbed and ride 0.5 miles to the next intersection. You'll drop through a break in the bluff line before descending back towards the lake. Follow the winding trail along the lake before coming back to the intersection described earlier. Turn right to go back to the trailhead or ride another loop or two.

Lake Wilson is a great spot to get some peace and quite in the midst of town. There is no restroom or water on site. A pavilion with picnic tables is located adjacent to the trailhead. The boat launch is located at the far end of the dam. Try your hand at fishing if you like. Contact Steve Hatfield, Fayetteville Parks and Recreation Director, at 479-444-3471 for more information.

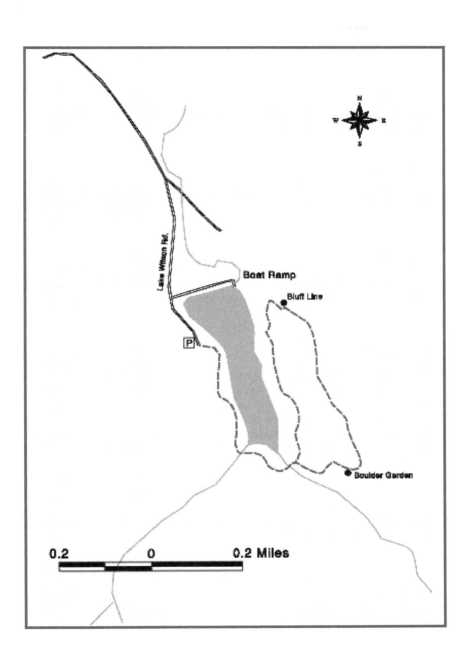

Devil's Den State Park

Easy / Intermediate

5

Trail length: 17+ miles
Ride time: Holt Road (1.5 - 2 hours), Fossil Flats (.5 - 1 hour)
Trail type: Loop trails with dirt road, double track, and singletrack

directions

Devil's Den State Park is located near Winslow, Arkansas. Starting in Fayetteville, AR, take Interstate 540 south to Hwy. 74. Turn right on Hwy. 74 and drive approximately 7 miles to Devil's Den State Park. The trailhead for the Holt Road Trail is on the left before you make the descent into the park. The parking area for the trail will be on the right. To get to the Fossil Flats Trail from the Visitors' Center, drive north on Hwy. 74. As soon as you cross the bridge over Lee Creek, turn right into Camp Area A. Fossil Flats Trail is located at the end of Camp Area A. Make sure to check in at the Visitors' Center before you ride the trails.

holt road loop

Holt Road Trail (12 miles) is the most well known trail in Arkansas. It's used as the cross-country course for the Arkansas State Mountain Bike Championships held every September. The trail is marked with brown bike signs over its entire length, but some intersections can still be confusing. Once on the trail, you will follow a dirt road downhill to the first intersection. Turn left and follow the old roadbed. This trail mostly follows the contour of the mountain. Turn right on a new logging road down to Blackburn Creek. When you reach the bottom, take a right and follow the trail downstream. You'll cross the creek twice before climbing up Quail Valley. This part of the trail becomes very steep and rocky. As you climb up Quail Valley, the trail gradually narrows down to a four-wheeler trail. Turn left onto a clearly marked section of singletrack just before you reach the top of the climb. You'll come out onto another four-wheeler trail for a short while before turning right onto more singletrack. Climb sharply uphill enjoy a short rest as the trail levels out on top of the ridge. You'll make your way through a few switchbacks before dropping quickly down to Holt Road. Turn left and follow the dirt road (Holt Road) uphill. This old roadbed will take you past an old homestead. This section of trail flows along the contour before descending to the intersection with the Butterfield trail. This section of trail is probably the most scenic. Look to your left and enjoy the view of Lee Creek Valley. Follow this trail back to Holt Road and turn left. Follow Holt Road on a long gradual incline back to the trailhead.

fossil flats trail

Fossil Flats Trail (3-5 miles) begins at the far end of Camp Area A. You'll start out on an old dirt road that is closed to traffic. Follow this road 1.25 undulating miles to the first intersection. This is where the short loop turns off. The short loop is only 3 miles. Continue on the dirt road if you are planning on doing the longer ride. The road climbs up in two short sections before leveling off and then dropping down to Lee Creek at 1.9 miles. After crossing the creek, you will come up to the next trail intersection. Turn right if you want to eliminate the climb. This will be a 4-mile loop.

entire trail

To do the whole trail, continue up the hill about 0.5 miles and then turn right onto singletrack. You'll know you're at the right spot when you see a small pond on the left. This is where the fun begins. Hold on tight as you follow a serpentine path through the woods for about a mile before it brings you out on the middle loop. Turn left at the intersection. You'll soon come out on a bluff line that overlooks Lee Creek. The scenery is beautiful, but riding can be treacherous. Exercise extreme caution on this section of trail. Follow the trail through the next drainage and bomb the descent back to the intersection with the short loop at 4.1 miles. Turn left and follow the trail to the next intersection. Turn left if you want to try the gravity cavity. Beginners should turn right. If you chose to ride the gravity cavity you'll pass through the hike-in campground for the Butterfield trail. Next, you will pass over a shale outcropping and ride down a long sandstone slab before crossing Lee Creek again to finish the ride. Pay attention to river levels before you attempt this ride.

Devil's Den State Park has 16 cabins with fireplaces and fully stocked kitchens. A café and pool are available during the summer. A park store offers groceries, gifts, and snacks. There are 148 campsites available in the park. Many sites offer water and electric hook ups. There's even a coin-operated laundry located next to the Visitor Center. For more information or to reserve a site, contact: Devil's Den State Park, 11333 West AR 74, West Fork, AR 72774. E-mail the park at devilsden@arkansas.com or dial 479-761-3325.

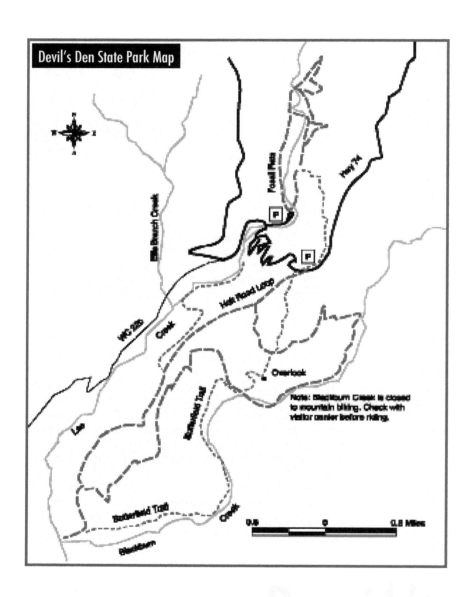

Devil's Den State Park Map

Fossil Flats

Hwy 74

Elk Branch Creek

Hale Road Loop

WG 20

Creek

Overlook

Rumbolsr Trail

Note: Blackburn Creek is closed to mountain biking. Check with visitor center before riding.

Loop

Butterfield Trail

Creek

Blackburn

0.8   0   0.8 Miles

Hobbs State Park Conservation Area

Easy / Intermediate

Trail length: 17 miles
Ride time: 30 minutes – 3 hours
Trail type: Singletrack; stacked loop system

directions

Hobbs State Park is located just east of Rogers, AR. From Interstate 540, exit on Hwy. 102/62 east. Turn left on Hwy. 62 east towards Rogers. Turn right on 2nd Street. Turn left on Prairie Creek Rd. (Hwy. 12). Follow Hwy. 12 to Hobbs State Park. The Van Winkle Trailhead will be on the right. The new Visitors' Center will be another 1.5 miles on the right. The War Eagle Trailhead will be on the left if you turn right (south) on War Eagle Road off Hwy. 12.

trail description

Hobbs State Park offers mountain bikers the newest trail system in the state. The trails are scheduled to open in 2005Y after the trailheads are completed Hwy. 12, Piney Road, and Townsend Ridge Road. Van Winkle Hollow offers riders an easy 1-mile trail along the valley floor. It's a great trail for beginners. More adventurous riders can explore routes off Piney Road and Townsend Ridge Road.

From the Piney Road Trailhead follow the singletrack west to your choice of two loops. You'll cross an access road and an old rusted out truck before you reach the trail intersection. Follow the trail to the left to do the skinny loop or to the right to take on the fat loop. The skinny loop drops down a narrow ridge and culminates with a spur trail that overlooks Beaver Lake. Keep your eyes open for bald eagles from December through February. Don't get too comfortable, there's a long climb back to the Fat loop. The Fat loop drops into Blackburn Hollow, which has some impressive moss-covered rock outcroppings. The climb out of Blackburn is fairly challenging. I prefer to ride the loop clockwise, but it can be ridden in either direction.

The two trails that connect Piney and Townsend Ridge Road offer riders a 10-mile loop. Starting from the trailhead on Townsend Ridge Road, you'll follow a short connection trail to the main loop. Turn right at the first intersection and immediately cross Townsend ridge road. You'll descend for a while before climbing around the top of two hollows. Future trail plans will offer a loop down to War Eagle, but the park needs to purchase some private property that dissects the planned route. Keep your eyes open to the right in this section. When the leaves are off, there are some great views of War Eagle Valley. Cross a small access road before climbing up and meeting Townsend Ridge Road again. On the other side of the road you'll work your way across a small ridge before the long, hair-raising descent down to Van Winkle Hollow. Take extra precaution on the decent, it is narrow and off camber to the downhill side. Cross a substantial bridge over Van Winkle Creek and start the switchback climb up the other side. When the trail reaches Piney Road it veers to the left and follows the road for a while. This section of trail sweeps into and out off the high side of several hollows, passes the trail connection to the trails on the west side of Piney road, and begins the long descent down to Van Winkle Hollow again. Let go of those breaks and let yourself rail the corners. Cross another bridge at the bottom and begin your climb up to Townsend Ridge Road. Look to your right as you climb out of the valley. There is a very large beaver pond. Follow this trail all the way back to the Townsend Ridge Trailhead. At the time of publishing, the trail along War Eagle Road has not been built. Visit the Visitor's Center before your next visit to get the latest information

Hobbs State Park—Conservation Area is unique in that it's managed by several different agencies, including Arkansas State Parks, Arkansas Heritage Commission, and Arkansas Game and Fish. Hobbs is the only State Park that allows hunting, so make sure to wear hunters' orange during the hunting seasons for bear, deer, and turkey, which are primarily during the late Fall and Spring. Trails are open to equestrians and hikers, so please be courteous of other trail users. For more information, contact Hobbs State Park at 479-789-2380.

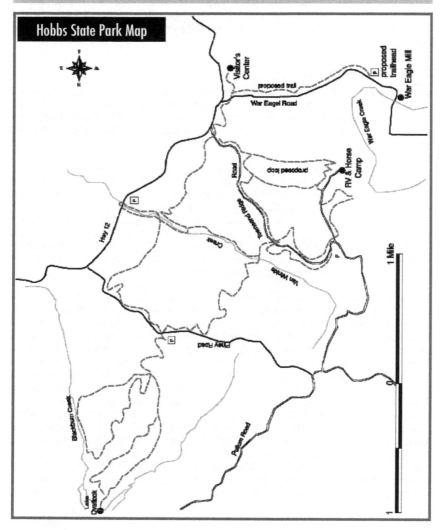

Lost Bridge Village - North

Intermediate

<u>Trail length</u>: 5 miles
<u>Ride time</u>: 45 minutes – 1 ¼ hours
<u>Trail type</u>: singletrack

directions

This trail is located on the north shore of Beaver Lake near Garfield. From Rogers, take Hwy. 62 east 12 miles to Garfield, AR or you can reach Garfield from the east by driving from Eureka Springs. Turn south on Hwy. 127, and drive 5.9 miles to Marina Rd. Turn left on Marina Rd. and enter Lost Bridge Park North. The trailhead is located on the right side of the road as you travel downhill towards the marina.

trail description

The trail at Lost Bridge Park offers mountain bikers a great opportunity to see parts of the park that most visitors choose to ignore. The best way to ride the trail is counter-clockwise. From the trailhead, immediately cross the road, walk up the steps, and begin your ride on the singletrack that starts on your right. You'll ride through a picnic area, so be aware of other park users and slow down. You'll follow the contour of the hill in the first mile before shouldering your bike for a short walk up a section of steps along a bluff. This area is very scenic, so take the time to enjoy your surroundings. Climb up a steep drainage before cutting back sharply to the left. You'll soon arrive at Marina Road. Continue to the other side of the road for the best part of the trail. You'll negotiate several switchbacks, and descend steeply down the mountain. You'll pass a small pond on your left before continuing along the bench. Weave along the hillside below a nearly continuous bluff. The Schrader homestead with chimney and part of the foundation still intact will be on your right as you make your way down the trail. Continue along the hillside past a walk-in campground and a spring. After riding around and over a fairly rocky and challenging section of trail, turn left and descend sharply down to the lake. This section of trail dips and rises several times, and is a particularly challenging section of trail. Skirt the lake all the way back to the trailhead. I would not recommend this trail for beginners, even though the trail is fairly short. Riders may consider climbing the paved road and riding the trail mostly downhill on both sides.

Lost Bridge Park is managed by the U.S. Army Corps of Engineers. The park offers a marina, campsites, swimming beach, and picnic areas. There are 48 campsites, ranging from $13-15 per night. Hot showers and drinking water are available. The fee season for the park is from April 1st to October 31st. Day use fees are $2. For more information about the park, contact the Beaver Lake Project Office at 479-636-1210. The main Beaver Lake office is located at 2260 N. 2nd St., Rogers, AR 72756.

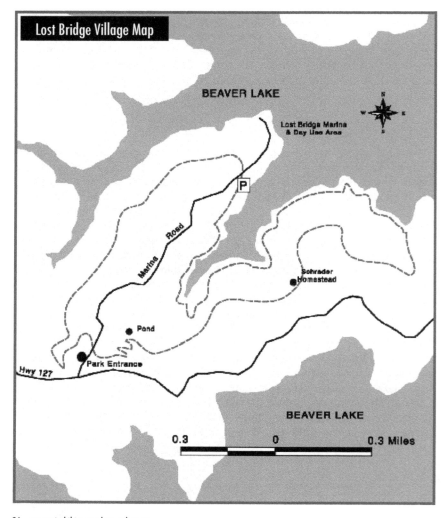

Madison Co. WMA

Intermediate / Difficult

Trail length: Loops range from 11 to 13 miles
Ride time: 1 ¼ -3 hours
Trail type: Dirt roads, double track, and singletrack

directions

The Wildlife Management Area (WMA) is located 12 miles north of Huntsville on Hwy. 23, or 13 miles south of Eureka Springs. Loops 1 and 2 start at the WMA Headquarters on the west side of the WMA. You can reach Loop 3 by traveling on County Rd. 30 (dirt road) approximately 7 miles to Rockhouse Church.

loop 1

Loop 1 (11 miles) starts at the WMA Headquarters on the west side. From the Headquarters, travel west on County Rd. 30 for 0.4 miles. Cross the gate and follow the old road bed to the north. When you intersect with another gravel road in 2 miles, turn right. Climb uphill for 0.6 miles and turn left through a wire gate. Follow this trail for 1.2 miles to the next intersection. You'll pass some really beautiful bluffs and waterfalls (below you). Follow the road to your left and take the first left again. Follow this trail for another 1.2 miles. There will be about 0.3 miles of hike-a-bike in this section. Turn left at this intersection and follow the dirt road back to County Rd. 30. Turn left on County Rd. 30 and follow the road to the east for 1 mile past Camp Area 5 and to Camp 7. Turn right (south) on this road and follow it for 0.15 miles to a trail that spurs to the right. Ride down a steep, rocky descent that skirts a stream. You'll follow the stream about 2 miles to Camp Areas 1 and 2. Explore the cave on your right before heading north on the road back to the HQ. It's only 2 miles back to your car.

loop 2

Loop 2 (12.5 miles) starts at Camp Area 7 about 2.6 miles east of Hwy. 23. Head south on the dirt road 0.15 miles to a trail that spurs to the right. There will be a wire across the trail. Follow the trail 2 miles to Camp Areas 1 and 2. Turn left on the dirt road to the south. Follow the road about 0.7 miles until the road T's. Turn left. Follow the road as it goes down the valley along Pine Creek for 0.8 miles, then turn left on the dirt road and climb up the hill. Follow this road for 1.7 miles to a faint trail on your right. Follow this trail past Camp 9 about 0.5 miles and turn right on the dirt road. Go down the road 0.6 miles to the intersection at Camp 10 and turn left. Follow this trail uphill 0.9 miles and turn right on M.C. 1254. Ride along M.C. 1254 to the intersection with WMA 447-19 and turn left. Camp 14 is straight ahead. WMA 447-19 continues downhill to the left and crosses a deep mud hole/creek. On the other side follow the four-wheeler trail east to the Kings River Scenic Overlook. During the winter, you can expect to see bald eagles in this area. Follow the trail you came in on back 0.6 miles and turn right (avoiding the mud hole). Follow this trail 0.9 miles uphill to the dirt road (1254) and turn right. Follow 1254 to 1230 (do not take the road on the right) to the north for 1.2 miles to the main dirt road (County Rd. 30). Turn left and return to Camp 7.

wildlife management area

loop 3

Loop 3 (13 miles) begins your ride at the white church in Rockhouse, which is located approximately 7 miles east of Hwy. 23. From the church, head west on the dirt road in front of you. Climb the hill approximately 2.3 miles to the top and turn left onto the dirt road trace. Follow this road 2.5 miles to Camp 21. Turn left and follow 447-8. Turn right at the first intersection and ride through several meadows towards Rockhouse Creek. Before you reach the creek, you'll enter a large food plot. Follow the edge of the plot on the left to a faint trail. This might require a little bushwhacking. The trail eventually takes you to Kettle Falls, which is truly spectacular. You'll understand why the fall got its name when you arrive. Bushwhack a short distance uphill to the east and turn right on the narrow road trace. You'll round the hillside and climb steeply up to an intersection. Turn right and ride downhill. Take your time riding this section. It is extremely washed out. Turn left at the bottom and climb past Camp 18 to Camp 19. You turn right and continue downhill again before the final climb back to the main road. Turn right and descend back to the church at Rockhouse. This trail route requires solid navigation skills. A topographic map of the area and compass is highly recommended.

Information: The Madison County WMA is one of the largest state-owned wildlife areas in Arkansas. The area is located in the Ozark Mountains with many steep mountains and narrow valleys. The trails can be very rocky, but they drain well and are rideable when other trails should be avoided. Major points of interest include the Kings River, Kings River Scenic Overlook, and Kettle Falls. The area is heavily hunted for deer during modern gun season from mid-November to early January and again in April for turkey, so please avoid the trails during this time. For more information about the WMA, contact Bob Wilson at 479-789-5262 or 479-264-4860.

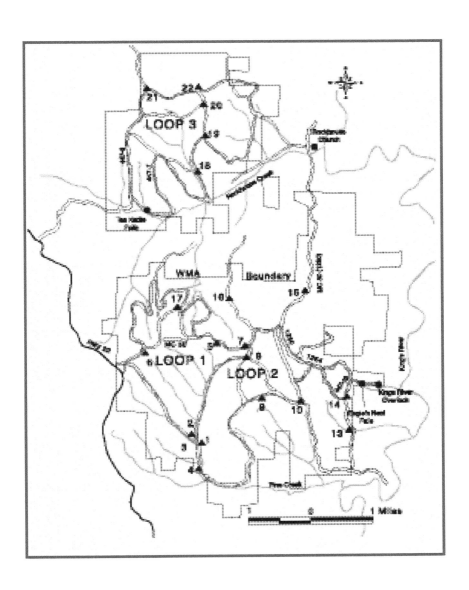

Lake Leatherwood Trail System

Intermediate

Trail length: 16+ miles total
Ride time: 30 minutes – 2 ½ hours
Trail type: Stacked loop system, doubletrack, and singletrack

directions

Lake Leatherwood Park is located 2 miles west of Eureka Springs off of Hwy. 62. Turn right into the Leatherwood park entrance and proceed to the parking area next to the bathhouse. All of the trails are accessible from this area.

trail description

Lake Leatherwood is a true mountain bike destination. Miles of quality singletrack will make you think twice about returning home. There is a little something to offer ever level of rider. Beginners can enjoy the Leatherwood Creek loop, which can be accessed from the ball field or Meadow trailhead. Intermediate loops include the Beacham and Fuller Trails that circle the lake. For the more challenging trails, check out the Miner's Rock, Dam Overlook, and Twin Knobs trails. Miner's Rock loop has several natural features along the trail, including its name sake rock, numerous limestone bluffs, and several sinkholes. Head up Mulladay Hollow to visit one of Lake Leatherwood's natural springs. Don't forget to check out Hyde Hollow Trail, which offers a scenic alternate route to the Twin Knobs Trail.

miner's rock trail

The Miner's Rock Trail (4 miles) is one of the more popular trails in the park. Begin at the Meadow trailhead. Ride southwest down the trail over two bridges that cross Leatherwood Creek. Turn right on the valley road (Leatherwood Creek Trail) passing the Twin Knobs trail intersection and continue 0.4 miles to the paved road. Take a left and a quick right onto the Miner's Rock Trail. The trail climbs up a new section of singletrack trail that switchbacks up the hill. After climbing about 0.5 mile, you will pass Miner's Rock, a large wave-like rock that rises 15-25 feet into the air. Continue up the hill and take the second road to the right. You will soon pass a power line and hit some singletrack. Follow the trail along the contour of the mountain. There are plenty of beautiful rock outcroppings along the way. Just before the trail hits another old roadbed, you will pass a sinkhole, which is on the left. The trail turns into singletrack again and rides along before you head downhill to the paved park road. Turn left on the paved road and turn left again to ride under the bridge and down Mulladay Hollow Creek back to the start at the Meadow trailhead. *Note: The upper part of Miner's Rock Trail is closed near the powerline, because the trail was built onto private property. The area is clearly marked, so please avoid this section of trail.

twin knobs trail

The Twin Knobs Trail (4.5 miles) is one of the more challenging trails in the park. It has several steep climbs that will test even the most experienced riders. Start at the Meadow trailhead. Follow the trail over the two bridges crossing Leatherwood Creek and turn right on the valley road (Leatherwood Creek Trail). The Twin Knobs Trail system will climb up to the left at 0.3 miles. If you cross a creek, you have gone too far. Follow the trail as it switchbacks up the hill. You will eventually come to the Bench Loop Trail. A trail kiosk is located here. Follow the trail to the right. The trail will follow the contour of the mountain for a while before climbing up to an old road bed. Follow this long bench below numerous rock outcroppings and a limestone bluff. This area is extremely scenic. As you round the hill turn right at the intersection and climb steeply to the top of the hill. You'll top both of the knobs before coming out on a dirt road. Turn left on the road and hold on tight for a very steep decent to your next intersection. Turn right onto the singletrack. This section of trail switchbacks downhill, then surfs the contours all the way back to kiosk at the bottom of the steep descent. There will be an opportunity to turn right halfway along the bench. The Hyde Hollow Trail is a scenic connection to the Beacham Trail. If you choose to ride to the kiosk, follow the same trail you climbed earlier trail back to the Meadow trailhead.

beacham/fuller trail

The Beacham/Fuller Trail (4 miles) is the first developed trail at Lake Leatherwood. This trail is an intermediate friendly trail with a few short technical sections. Start at the Fuller trailhead near the boat ramp. Then ride an undulating section of trail above the lake for about a mile before you arrive at the Point Camp road. If you turn right, you'll terminate at a point with a view of the dam. Continue straight on the trail for another half mile and you'll come out on the access road to the dam. Turn right and ride a short distance to the dam. Cross the dam and follow the trail to the right. You'll pass directly through the limestone quarry used for the dam construction. Take some time to enjoy the views of the lake on your left. You'll pass the Hyde Hollow, which will be the third drainage on the right. You'll climb and descend several times before returning to Leatherwood Creek. Follow the trail to the right over two bridges and back to the Meadow trailhead. Continue up the road to the parking area where you began.

dam overlook trail

The Dam Overlook Trail (4 miles) is a challenging trail that offers trail users a commanding view of Lake Leatherwood. Start at the meadow below the bathhouse. Follow Mulladay Hollow upstream past the stone bridge. After about 0.25 miles, the trail will switchback up the hill before leveling out on an old road bed. An old four wheeler trail comes up from the right. Continue following the trail along the contour for about 0.3 miles and turn left on the singletrack. If you start to head downhill, you've gone too far. You will circle around the hollow below a beautiful bluff and come out at the dam overlook. The dam is only visible when the leaves are off the trees. Follow the roadbed down the hill. Turn left at the first intersection you came to. After following the road trace for a short distance, there will be a singletrack trail that goes down the hill to the right. Follow this fun little section of trail down to the Beacham Trail (dirt road). Turn right and ride along the dirt road to the trailhead. Another option is to come back on the Fuller Trail. This adds a little more singletrack to the ride.

Dave Renko rides past a scenic view of Lake Leatherwood on the Fuller Trail.

Lake Leatherwood City Park is located on the outskirts of Eureka Springs. This 1,600-acre park encompasses a 100-acre lake with the largest hand-laid limestone dam in the nation. The Beacham Trail travels over the top of the dam. The park features breathtaking natural beauty. Eureka Springs welcomes mountain bikers to the area. Most of the trails in the park were designed, maintained, and built by the Ozark Off Road Cyclists and local volunteers. The park also offers cabins, camping, fishing, swimming, and boat rentals. For more information contact: Lake Leatherwood Park, 1303 CR 204, Eureka Springs, AR 72632 or call 479-253-8624. Individual trail maps are available at the park office next to the boat ramp.

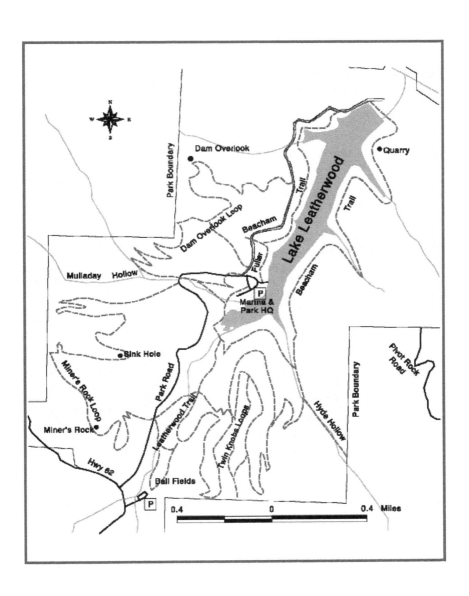

Mill Creek Trail System
Easy / Difficult

Trail length: 27-mile outer loop; 15 miles of inner loops
Ride time: 3-4 hours outer loop; 30 minutes — 2 hours inner loops
Trail type: Double track and 4-wheeler trails

directions
From Fayetteville, take Hwy. 16 east approximately 26 miles to Combs. Turn right on Forest Service Road 1007 for 4 miles. Turn left on FS Road 1509. Then go 0.5 miles to the trailhead. The trailhead is on the left side of the road. From Ozark, take Hwy. 23 north to Cass. Follow Forest Service Road 1520 west 8 miles to FS Road 1509, then turn north and drive 4 miles to the trailhead.

trail description
The Mill Creek Trail System is open to mountain bikers, 4-wheelers, and horseback riders. The 26-mile outer loop(M), marked with blue blazes, is the most difficult. After crossing Mill Creek turn left on the warm-up loop. You'll ride on the hillside above Mill Creek for a short distance, cross a drainage, then begin a long climb up the flanks of Burrell Mountain. Before reaching the top you'll drop over the ridge and descend down several switchbacks to McHone Creek. After crossing the creek you'll begin a long climb up Allard Mountain. You'll circle around the edge of the mountain after you reach the top. There are some amazing views of the surrounding Ozark National Forest from this mountain. Next, you'll follow a pipeline for a while and descend an eroded section of trail back to McHone Creek (you may need to walk this section). Ride upstream along McHone Creek, then gradually climb to the top of Burrell Mountain again. You have the option to take one of the shortcuts back to the trailhead or you can ride the loop around the top of Burrell Mountain(B). If you continue forward, you' drop down to Fisher Hollow before climbing up again to a narrow ridge. Follow the ridge south for a while before making the last descent to Mill Creek. Enjoy the downhill along Mill Creek all the way back to the trailhead.

There are several options for shorter loops if you utilize the shortcuts (C) shown on the map. The Warm-up loop, marked with a D, is a good way to gage you abilities if you are new to riding. Trails should be avoided when they are wet. Mill Creek Trail System is heavily used by 4-wheelers and motorcycles so expect to see other people on the trail.

There is a vault toilet and information board located at the trailhead. No campsites are available next to the trail. White Rock Mountain Recreation Area and Shores Lake offer established campsites, water, and other amenities. Contact the Boston Mountain Ranger District at 501-667-2191 for more information about the area. There is a gas station in Combs on Hwy. 16. The wild and scenic Mulberry River is located just south of Mill Creek on Hwy. 23. For more information about the Mulberry River, log on to www.turnerbend.com.

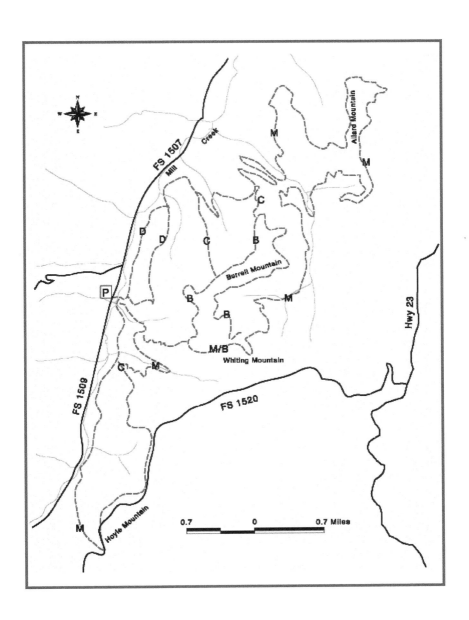

Moccasin Gap Trail System

11

Easy / Difficult

Trail length: 28 miles
Ride time: 30 minutes – 3 hours
Trail type: Stacked loop system; dirt roads

directions

The Moccasin Gap Trail System is located 23 miles north of Russelleville, AR. Starting at Interstate 40, turn north on Hwy. 7. Drive 23 miles north to the Moccasin Gap Trail. The trail is located on the west side of the road. The trail is clearly marked by a brown sign along Hwy. 7.

trail description

The Moccasin Gap Trail System utilizes old Forest Service roads that weave through the rugged Ozark Mountains. This multi-use trail system is open to horses, motorized vehicles, and mountain bikes, so please yield the trail when encountering other trail users. All the trails are well marked and easy to follow. Each loop has a color-coded horseshoe shaped symbol placed prominently on trees at eye level. In addition to the tree markings, there are brown posts at each trail intersection that have letters that match the trail map.

beginner loop

There are two beginner loops that begin from the parking area. The first is a 2.8 mile loop that leaves directly from the parking area. Follow the trail to the left along the ridge to (G) at 1.3 miles. Turn right and ride 0.2 miles to (F). Complete the loop by turning right and riding 1.3 miles to the parking area. Another 2 mile loop can be added on to this trail by turning left at (G) and riding 0.6 mile to (H). Descend down 0.3 miles to Stave Mill Creek (I). You'll pass the two waterfalls on the way to (E). Turn right and climb 0.3 miles back to (F) to complete the loop. This trail will connect you to the Stave Mill Falls Loop and The Black Oak Ridge Loop.

34   mountain biking northern arkansas

stave mill falls loop

The Stave Mill Falls Loop (4.5 miles) a great loop for intermediate riders that passes two beautiful waterfalls. From the parking area ride out the ridge about 1.3 miles to the intersection (G) and turn right. Ride 0.5 miles to the intersection with the Stave Mill Falls Loop at intersection (E). Turn left and follow Stave Mill Creek to the waterfalls. Turn right at the (I) intersection and climb 0.7 miles up to the overlook at intersection (J). Descend 0.5 miles down to (L) turn right and continue to 0.3 miles to (M). Follow Mocassin Creek downhill 0.5 miles to the (N) intersection and turn right. Climb 0.6 miles up past the intersection of Stave Mill Hollow and Gap Hollow to (C) and turn right. Continue another 0.6 miles to (D). You'll top a ridge before completing the loop at (E).

black oak ridge loop

You will have to ride about 3 miles of trail before you can make the connection with the Black Oak Ridge Loop (3.5 miles). Starting at the (J) intersection turn left and ride 1.2 mile to the intersection with (K). You ride about 0.1 miles and the trail will drop down into Mocassin Hollow for a 1.7 mile descent to the intersection with (L). Turn right and climb 0.5 miles up to complete the loop.

high mountain inner and outer loops

You'll need to ride about 4.5 miles utilizing the beginner trail and Stave Mill Falls Loop to reach the High Mountain Loops (13.9 miles). You'll reach the Outer High Mountain loop at intersection (M) along Mocassin Creek. Turn left at (M) and ride 0.6 mile to (R). Turn right and climb 0.7 miles up to the Inner High Mountain Loop or follow the trail to the left and climb 1.8 miles to the intersection with (O). Turn left and descend towards Mocassin Creek. You'll ride 7.4 miles before you connect with the Stave Mill Falls Loop at (N). Continue to the right to complete the Outer Loop (10.6 miles). The 3.3 mile Inner High Mountain Loop is a nice addition, if you want to ride all of the trails. This trail is for experienced riders only.

gap hollow loop

The Gap Hollow Trail (3.5 miles) can be reach by riding north out of the parking area 0.8 miles to intersection (B). Turn right and follow the trail 2.1 miles down to the bottom of Gap Hollow (C). Turn left and climb 0.6 miles up to (D). Turn left and return to (B) after climbing an additional 0.8 miles. The Stave Mill Falls loop is a perfect connector trail for intermediate and experienced riders.

Seventeen campsites are available near the trailhead. There is a pit toilet, water, and trashcans on site. Gas, groceries, and showers are available at Mack's Pines, located 2 miles south of the main entrance on Hwy. 7. For more information about the trail and the surrounding Ozark National Forest, contact the Bayou Ranger District at 501-284-3150.

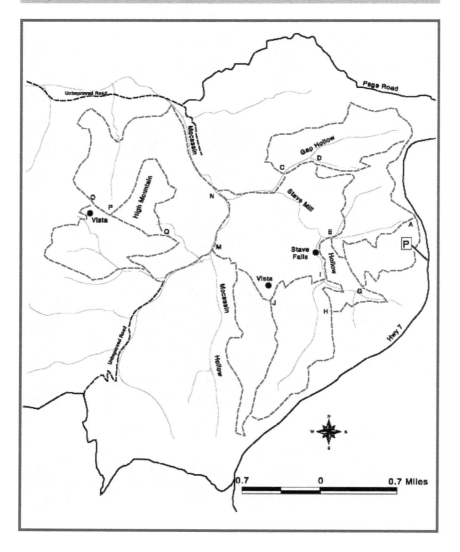

Pigeon Creek Trail System

Intermediate

12

Trail length: 25 miles
Ride time: 20 minutes – 2 ½ hours
Trail type: Stacked loop system; singletrack

directions

The Pigeon Creek Trail System is located 6 miles north of Mountain Home on Hwy. 201. The west trailhead is located on the left side of the road as you head north from Mountain Home. The east trailhead is located on the right side of the road just north of the west trailhead.

trail description

The Pigeon Creek System is one of the only National Recreational Trails designated in Arkansas. The trails are well marked with brown carcinite signs, routed wooden signs, and plastic markers on trees.

100 series trails

The trails on the east side of Hwy. 201 are marked with the 100 series trail signs (15 miles). From the parking lot, trail 100 offers riders a challenging loop that climbs up and over the ridge adjacent to Hwy. 201. Trail 101 is an excellent connector trail to loops 104, 105, and 106. You'll cross several drainages before climbing up to the connection with 102. You can stay up high on this section to ride 102 or drop down to ride 103. Trail 103 has a sharp dip close to the lake that will get your adrenaline going. Trails 102 and 103 can be ridden as a loop or as part of a larger loop including the previously mentioned trails. Once you've made the climb up to 104 you'll pass a great scenic overlook of Norfork Lake. Take a few moments to enjoy the view before descending a series of switchbacks and continue your loop around the ridge to the intersection with 105. Trail 105 takes you out on the flats along the lake. You'll come out on a road. Turn right and climb for a little while before you begin Trail 106. Trail 106 is one of the more challenging loops on the trail. You'll descend and climb several times before topping the ridge and connecting with trail 102. Follow 102 back to 101 and the trailhead.

200 series trails

The trails on the west side of the road have a 200 series numbering system (10 miles). Trails 201 and 202 are the most beginner friendly trail in the park. Both of these trails offer short loops that stay close to Norfork Lake. Trail 203 climbs steeply up to the top of the hill and connects with an unnumbered trail further to the west. This trail is extremely challenging and should not be attempted by beginner riders. You'll follow the contour along the hillside for a short distance before coming to the bluff. Make sure you walk down the steps to a narrow section of trail above Pigeon Creek. This area is beautiful. After you've made it through this difficult section you'll travel northwest up the valley to a dirt road. Cross the creek and climb up the other side. The trail is fairly challenging through this section with lots of short steep pitches and rock ledges. You'll descend down a set of switchbacks after riding out a long ridge.

After the descent, cross Pigeon Creek again and return to the trailhead. This trail may not be accessible when the lake is at high levels. Check with the Corps of Engineers office to get the latest trail conditions.

The trails at Pigeon Creek were designed and built by the Twin Lakes Bike Club based out of Mountain Home. The trail system is open to bicycle and hiking traffic year-round. Horses and/or any kind of motorized vehicle are not permitted on the trails. Fires and cutting of firewood is prohibited, firearms are not allowed in the park, and littering is strictly against the law. There is no water or restrooms on site. The Cranfield campground is located on the south side of the lake. It can be reached from Hwy. 412/62. Mountain Home is located just 6 miles south of the trails on Hwy. 201. There are plenty of restaurants and hotels available in town. For more information about the area, contact the U.S. Army Corps of Engineers at 870-425-2700.

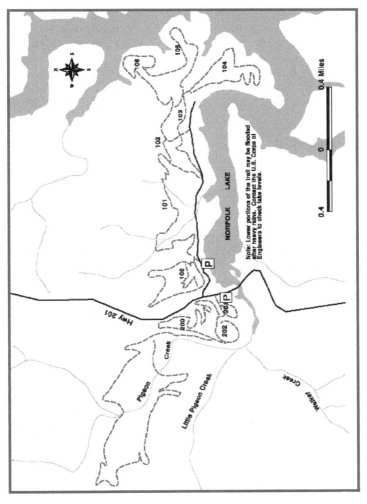

Syllamo Trail System

Intermediate

Trail length: 39 miles
Ride time: 30 minutes to 6 hours
Trail type: Stacked loop system; singletrack and double track

directions

The Syllamo trailhead is located on Hwy. 5 approximately 4.75 miles north of the community of Allison. From the south, Allison is located 5.5 miles north of Mountain View on Hwy. 5. Coming from the north, Allison is about 41 miles south of Mountain Home on Hwy. 5. The White River Bluff Trailhead located 1.5 miles west of Highway 5 on Green Mountain Road. The Scrappy Mountain trailhead is another 3 miles down Green Mountain Road from there. The trail can also be accessed from Blanchard Springs campground off Hwy. 14 west of Allison.

white river bluff loop

The White River Bluff Loop (4.5 miles) is located off Green Mountain Road a 1.5 miles west of Hwy. 5. The trail is easily followed by using the green color-coded trail markers. The singletrack starts right from the trailhead. You'll cross a dirt road before coming to the actual loop. The trail can be ridden in either direction, but I prefer to ride it counterclockwise. Turn right at the intersection and cross the road again. You'll climb up to a ridge top and follow it around to a small hollow. You'll descend down a steep section of old roadbed and cross an access road before climbing again. The trail winds through a pine grove and pops out on a narrow ridge. Keep your eyes pealed for the view on the right. You'll descend down through a rock garden before coming out at the overlook. Take a few minutes to gaze down the White River Valley. Back on the trail, you'll drop down a couple switchbacks and follow the hillside back to the trailhead.

bald scrappy loop

The Bald Scrappy Loop (7.3 miles) is marked by orange trail markings. The best place to begin your ride is from the White River Bluff Trailhead. Again the best way to ride this loop is counterclockwise. You'll begin your ride directly across Green Mountain Road. You'll parallel Green Mountain Road down the mountain for a hair-raising descent. The best part of the descent is right at the top when you roll down a 10-foot rock slab. At the bottom you'll take a quick left and follow an old 4-wheeler trail for a while. You'll climb and descend a couple times before a wicked fast descent to an old roadbed. Turn left and make a quick right on another roadbed before hitting the singletrack again. You'll climb all the way back to the shared orange/blue trail. You'll cross a road then make a steady climb up Bald Scrappy Mountain to the top. You'll roll right over several sections of exposed sandstone. You'll cross Green Mountain Road and descend down to the last section of singletrack. On the way down you'll pass a cairn for Shawn Ausburn, a Fayetteville mountain biker, who passed away while riding the trail. Turn left at the next intersection and ride the last bit of singletrack back to the trailhead.

scrappy mountain loop

The Scrappy Mountain Loop (12 miles) is marked with blue trail markers. Begin your ride from the Syllamo trailhead on Hwy.5. The climbing will be intense no matter which direction you choose. Starting in a clockwise direction, you'll immediately cross Highway 5. You'll follow the blue markers along the highway to your left, then climb steeply towards the road. Right before you reach the road, the trail cuts back to the right (It's easier to miss than you think). The trail then crosses Livingston Creek on solid bedrock. The trail skirts a pasture and begins the long climb up over Bald Scrappy Mountain. After you finish the blue/orange section you'll turn to the right on the singletrack. This section of trail is a mountain biker's dream. Flowing trail with great scenery and plenty of rock ledges, chutes, and pinches that will keep you on your toes. The trail eventually climbs its way up to the intersection with the Blanchard Springs Loop (Yellow). Ride along the blue/yellow trail for a short distance past the Scrappy Mountain Trailhead. You'll climb steady for a little while before crossing the road. Follow the unmaintained road on the other side for a super fast descent. When you reach the singletrack again, the trail follows the ridge again and gradually becomes rockier until you reach the "stairway to heaven." More advanced riders can ride this rock stairway through a break in the bluff. If you don't feel comfortable, don't ride it. Enjoy the descent all the way to Hwy. 5. You're not done yet. The trail crosses the road and climbs up again. Watch out for a tight switchback on the way up that forces most riders to dismount. The trail continues to climb further until you finally top out and follow an old four wheeler trail. You'll intersect a dirt road and turn right and finish the ride with an exhilarating drop back to the trailhead.

blanchard springs loop

Blanchard Springs Loop (15 miles), marked with yellow, is the newest addition to the Syllamo Trail System. Begin your ride from Scrappy Mountain Trailhead on Green Mountain Road or start directly from Blanchard Springs Caverns off Hwy. 14. If you start from Blanchard Spring campground, you'll begin a long climb up a narrow valley. You'll pass a connecting trail (green marker) further up the mountain (I would not recommend riding up). Cross a dirt road that connects Green Mountain Road to Blanchard Springs (closed to vehicles) and continue to climb all the way up to the top. After crossing Green Mountain Road the trail follows the contours on a section of super smooth trail. Cross Green Mountain Road again and continue to the Blue/Yellow trail. After intersecting with the blue/yellow, enjoy the descent down to the next trail intersection. You'll begin my favorite section of trail in the whole area. The trail descends for a while and follows the contour weaving through sections of exposed limestone rock. Turn right onto a 4-wheeler trail for a short distance before jumping back into the singletrack. Climb up to an impressive overlook of the Sylamore River Valley. Huge limestone bluffs thrust up from the river, making this an excellent stop on an epic ride. After a snack and a short break, climb up through a few boulders to the ridgeline. Once on top you'll follow a 4-wheeler trail for quite a while over several long climbs. The singletrack will eventually start again on the right, and begin the long ride back to the campground. You'll pass through two large valleys on your way back before reaching the green connector trail I mentioned earlier. Turn left here if you want to shorten your ride, otherwise continue through the next valley before the long descent back to Blanchard Springs.

There is a vault toilet located at each trailhead. Blanchard Springs Caverns is located just 6 miles west of Allison and offers 32 campsites. There are 2 group campsites available by reservation only. There are also restrooms with hot showers, and drinking water is available. Allison has a restaurant and gas station. Mountain View, with all the comforts of home, is located just 6 miles from the trail system. While you're in the area, check out the Ozark Folk Center State Park, and float or fish the Buffalo and White Rivers. Take a guided tour into the spectacular Blanchard Springs Caverns. For more information about the trail system, contact the U.S. Forest Service office in Mountain View at 870-269-3228.

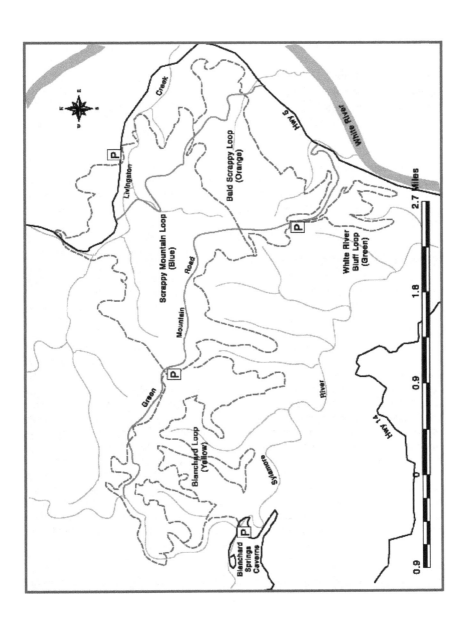

Springhill Park Trail

Easy

14

Trail length: 10 miles
Ride time: 1 - 2 hours
Trail type: Singletrack

directions

Springhill Park is located near Barling, Arkansas. From Interstate 40 near Van Buren, take Interstate 540 south 3 miles. Exit on Hwy. 59. Turn left and drive 7.5 miles south on Hwy. 59. Drive over the Arkansas River and continue to the Springhill Park entrance. Turn left into Springhill Park. The trailhead is located on your right as you drive into the park.

trail description

Springhill Park is one of two trails located along the Arkansas River. Most riders choose to ride the course counterclockwise, but it can be ridden in either direction. You'll begin the ride with a level, twisting section of trail directly south of the parking area. The trail meanders along the south side of the park, turns left along a pipeline for a short distance, and turn abruptly to the right back to singletrack. You'll follow the trail to the east to the far end of the park before making your way back. Watch out for the stinging nettles along the trail in the spring and summer. You'll pass through several sandy sections so control your speed before you enter them. Keep your eyes to the right, you'll start to see glimpses of the Arkansas River. You will cross the paved access road at the east end of the park and weave your way back to the road crossing again. You'll notice that the trailhead is on the left, before you pass through a campground. The trail stays close to the river for a little while before crossing another access road. Pass to the right of the play ground and follow the road for a short distance and cross the road again. Stay on the trail under Hwy. 59 bridge and follow the trail to the left on the other side. You'll cross the road again and loop through open woods to the north of the west campground. Cross the road again and complete the loop, before finishing up the last section. There are three main loops for the trail system. The outer loop is 10 miles long. Shorter loops range from 3 to 7 miles. The trail is well marked and easy to follow. Yellow markers with numbers located every 0.2 miles. Line of sight is fairly limited in sections, so stay alert and keep your bike under control.

Springhill Park is managed by the U.S. Army Corps of Engineers. The park offers campsites for tents and RVs ranging from $8-$14 per night depending on the services at the site. Warm showers available on the east and west ends of the park. Pavilions, picnic tables, playgrounds, and boat ramps available for park users. For more information about the park, contact the Ozark Field Office at 479-667-2129 or contact the park directly at 479-452-4598.

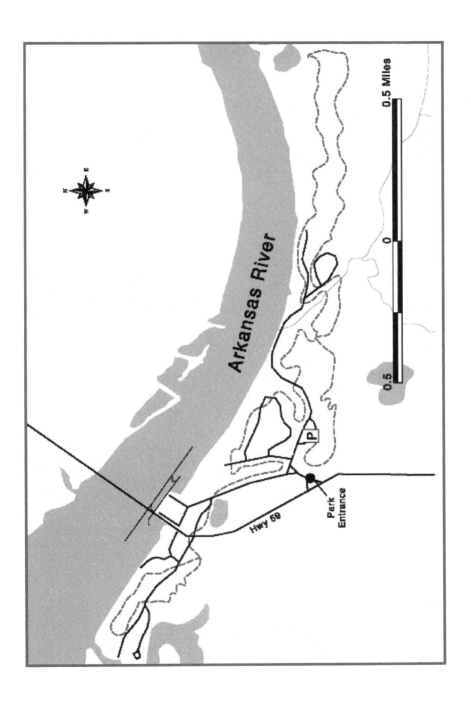

Huckleberry Mountain Trail System

Intermediate / Difficult

15

Trail length: 40 miles total; 29-mile Orange Loop and 11-mile White Loop
Ride time: 3 - 4 hours Orange Loop; 1½ - 2 hours White Loop
Trail type: singletrack, double track, and dirt roads

directions

The Huckleberry Mountain Trail System is located near Paris, AR. The White Trail can be accessed from the Mount Magazine State Park located off Hwy. 309 on Forest Road 1638. The trail starts at the camp, crosses Hwy. 309, and continues on the other side. The best place to start the orange loop is from Huckleberry Cap located on Forest Road 1613. From Paris, head south on Hwy. 309 about 11 miles to Forest Road 1601. Turn left, then continue 8 miles to Forest Road 1613. Turn left again and follow the road 3.5 miles to camp. Sorghum Hollow Camp can be reached via Forest Road 1614 south of Hwy. 22 at Midway.

trail description

The Huckleberry Mountain Trails are a multi-use trail system open to equestrians, mountain bikers, and hikers. These trails are located adjacent to Mt. Magazine, the highest point in Arkansas. Two loops offer up to 40 miles of trail in the Ozark National Forest.

orange loop

Beginning at Huckleberry camp, the Orange Trail (29 miles) descends down to Shoal Creek. Sorghum Hollow Camp will be on the right off Forest Road 1604. You'll cross Shoal Creek numerous times as you climb up the valley. Cross Forest Road 1601 and turn left at the trail intersection with the white trail. Follow Forest Road 1601 for nearly 2 miles before crossing the road and climbing up to 1613. Turn left on Forest Road 1613 and ride north for a short distance. A 9-mile shortcut is welcomed relief for tired legs. Turn right (east) on the trail aroung Huckleberry Mountain, if you want to complete the entire ride. You'll cross Forest Road 1613 one more time before returning to Huckleberry Camp.

white loop

The White Trail (11 miles) begins at Mount Magazine campground. This loop is challenging either way, but I prefer to ride the loop clockwise. After descending off Mount Magazine, drop down to Shoal Creek. When you reach the bottom, there is an option to turn left to ride the Orange loop. Turn right at the bottom and begin the climb up to Forest Road 1690, if you want to continue the White loop. Turn right at the next intersection with Forest Road 1612. Ride along the hillside for a short distance before dropping down to the upper reaches of Shoal creek and climb back

From April to May, a portion of the Orange Trail is closed for turkey hunting and nesting/hatching season. Camping is available at Mt. Magazine State Park, Sorghum Hollow Camp, and Huckleberry Camp. A vault toilet is available at the Sorghum Hollow Camp. The Huckleberry Camp is undeveloped. Mt. Magazine State Park offers water and campsites. For more information, contact the Magazine Ranger District at 501-963-3076.

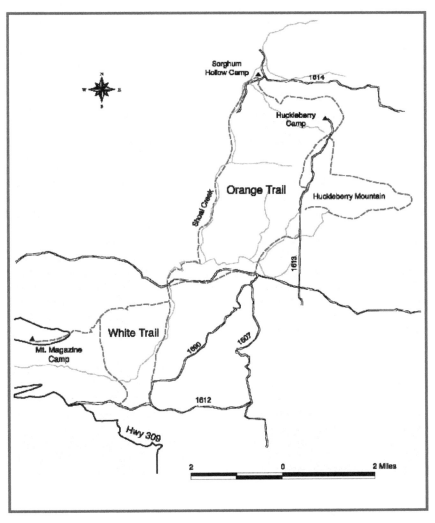

Mount Nebo Trail
Easy / Intermediate

16

Trail length: 4 miles
Ride time: 25-45 minutes
Trail type: dirt road loop

directions

This trail is located near Dardanelle, AR. From Interstate 40 in Russelleville, AR, drive south on Hwy. 7 approximately 7.5 miles to Hwy. 22. Turn right on Hwy. 22 and drive west 0.3 miles to Hwy. 155. Turn right on Hwy. 155 and drive 6 miles to Mt. Nebo State Park. The trailhead for the bench trail will be on your right as you go up the hill. A pavilion at the trailhead overlooks the Arkansas River Valley to the north.

trail description

The Mount Nebo Trail is a great trail for all levels of riders, but the trail is more suitable for beginner and intermediate abilities. The trail is actually an old roadbed that circles the mountain. You can ride the trail in either direction, but I'll describe the loop in a counterclockwise direction. You'll begin with a short climb that passes below the visitor's center. Keep your eyes open to the northeast when the leaves are off the trees. The views are stunning. Continue around the north end of the mountain and gradually descend to the backside of the mountain. You'll pass several streams, a pond, and an old foundation for a lodge. This is a great opportunity to explore a part of the past. Climb back on the bike, and continue uphill passing some unique rock outcroppings and a rockslide. Continue around the south side of the mountain below Sunrise Point. You'll enjoy a short section of fairly level trail before returning to Hwy. 155. Ride on the right side of the road back to the start near the overlook. If that wasn't enough distance for you, head up the hill on the paved road and check out sunrise and sunset points. The views are spectacular.

Mt. Nebo is one of Arkansas's most beautiful state parks. There are commanding views of the Arkansas River Valley to the north and the Ouachita Mountains to the south. There are over 14 miles of trails in the park. There are a wide variety of recreational activities available, including a swimming pool, tennis courts, playgrounds, and a ball field. The Visitor's Center and park store is located on the north side of the mountain. The park even offers bike rentals. There are 35 campsites at Mt. Nebo. Twenty-five sites offer electricity and water for $12/night. The remaining 10 are walk-in campsites for hikers for $6/night. Fifteen cabins with kitchen range from $78-124 per night. For more information, contact Mt. Nebo State Park at 479-229-3655. The address is #1 State Park Drive, Dardanelle, AR 72834.

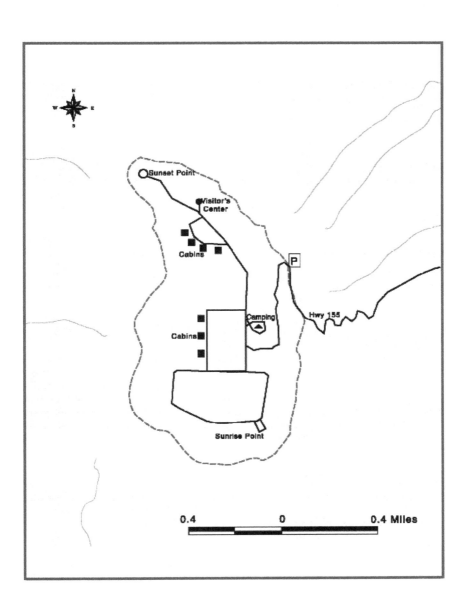

Old Post Trail

Easy / Intermediate

17

Trail length: 8 miles
Ride time: 30 minutes – 1 hour
Trail type: stacked loop system; singletrack and doubletrack

directions

From Interstate 40 in Russelleville, take Hwy. 7 south 4.6 miles to Lock and Dam Road. Turn right on Lock and Dam Rd. and drive 1.8 miles to the Dam Overlook Road. Turn right and drive to the Caudle Overlook. The trailhead sign will be on the right as you drive into the parking area.

trail description

The Old Post Trail offers riders a two mile beginner trail and a 6 mile intermediate trail. There is a kiosk at the trailhead that provides visitors a good overview of the trail system. The trail is not marked.

beginner loop

The beginner loop (2 miles) utilizes an old roadbed that makes a gently curving loop around the park. The road is wide enough for riders to ride side by side for short sections, but the road has some loose rocks and a few eroded sections. From the parking area, climb a gentle slope to the north. Pass all the singletrack options that leave the trail and continue the loop around the quarry. You'll follow the trail along the contour of the hill before descending down past the pond. Follow the trail to the right and complete the loop back to the parking lot.

intermediate loop

The intermediate loop (6 miles) starts to the left shortly after the beginning of the trail. Follow the trail as it twists back and forth across the hillside and crosses a powerline right-of-way. On the other side, you'll ride past the bluffs overlooking the Arkansas River to the southwest. You should be able to see the lock and dam here. Climb back to the east away from the river and ride a series of tight twisting trail that has some great, banked turns. The trail continues to the east just north of the quarry, connecting with the beginner trail for a short while before heading into the woods again. The trail cuts back and forth across a small stream, then cuts through the quarry. The trail pops out just to the north of a pond and parallels the road back to the trailhead.

The Old Post Park offers visitors 40 campsites with water and electricity for $16 per night. Playgrounds, picnic tables, restrooms, and drinking water available in the park. If you're lucky, you might see a large tanker make its way through the lock. You can thank the riders from Russelleville for getting permission to build the mountain bike trails at the park. The Corps of Engineers have been extremely open to mountain biking. For more information about the park, contact the Dardanelle Field Office at 479-968-5008. The office is located at 1598 Lock & Dam Road, Russelleville, AR 72801.

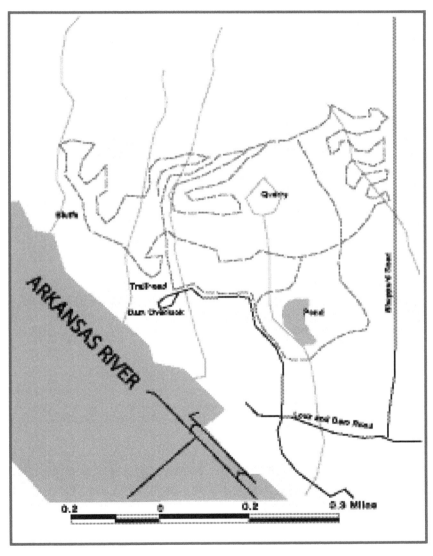

Camp Robinson Trail System
Easy / Intermediate / Difficult

18

Trail length: 35 + miles
Ride time: 30 minutes to 4 + hours
Trail type: Stacked loop system; singletrack

directions

Camp Robinson is located just north of Little Rock, AR. From Interstate 40, take the Burns Park exit and drive north on Military Drive about 3 miles to the base entrance. Follow the road into the base and turn left around the traffic circle. The Police Station is on the right on Arkansas Drive. Sign in before you head out to the trail. Return to Military Drive and turn left on Kansas Drive. The road will turn into Nebraska Drive as you head west. The parking lot will be on the left. The trails are located to the east of West Boundary Road.

trail description

Camp Robinson offers mountain bikers a wide variety of trail options. Most of the trails are singletrack. All of the trails are marked, but I would recommend first time riders bring a map until you feel more comfortable navigating the trail system. The easiest loops are located close to the main trail head, and grow progressively more challenging the farther out you ride.

pipeline and yucca trail

Beginners can start out on the Pipeline Trail (0.4 miles) just off West Boundary Road. From there, turn right on to the Yucca Trail (0.8 miles) . The Yucca Trail is a fairly smooth and fast section of trail that connects you to most of the trail system.

5-mile loop

5-mile Loop will be immediately on your left when you reach the Yucca Trail. There are two trail options on the 5-mile loops. Both trails stay primarily on top of the mountain, providing a challenge to all levels of riders. This trail is perfect for intermediate riders.

twin bridges loop, christmas tree loops and extension

Twin Bridges Loop (0.9 miles), Christmas Tree Loops (1 mile), and Christmas Tree Extension (0.9 miles) are great intermediate trails to link up with Yucca. Twin Bridges Loop is almost completely flat with short ups and downs. Christmas Tree Loop gets its name from a cedar tree that has been decorated with ornaments made from bicycle parts. Christmas Tree Extension is a more challenging trail that has some short steep

airport loop

The Airport Loop (1.7 miles)can be reached at the far end of the Yucca trail by turning right and riding a short distance on the dirt road. This loop is another excellent intermediate trail.

buddha and ball of nails

At the far end of the Airport Loop, advanced riders can tackle the Buddha (1.6 miles) and Ball of Nails (0.7 miles). Both of these trails offer up a heaping dose of rocky trail, exposure, tight twisting trail, and climbing.

porta potty and outer loop

After making your way around Ball of Nails don't forget to climb back up the dirt road to enjoy the Outer Loop (2.8 miles) and Porta Potty (1.6 miles). Strange names, but great trails! These trails are for intermediate to experienced riders just because of their distance from the trailhead and length. These two trails are my favorite trails at the camp.

elevator and lowlands

After finishing up Porta Potty, try taking the Elevator (0.5 miles) down to the Lowlands (1.6 miles) for a dose of mostly level, twisting singletrack. Intermediate riders can cut their teeth on a longer ride by checking out these trails. However, the elevator can be a punishing climb.

can of corn

The Can of Corn Trail (2.3 miles) can be reached by the gasline on the west side or near the end of the Elevator Trail. The trail meanders in the valley with little elevation change. This would be a great trail for beginners if it was a little closer to the trailhead. If you began the trail at the end of the Elevator, you'll complete the trail at the bottom of the gas line that dissects the trail system on the west side.

merlin's trail

Climb up the gas line and turn left to try your skills on Merlin's Trail (2.5 miles). You'll need a little magic to clean this section of trail without putting a foot down. Merlin twists and turns, climbing up and down the mountain several times through rocky terrain and off camber sections of trail. This trail is recommended only for experienced riders. As you finish up Merlin, turn right on the dirt road. Follow the access road to the southwest to the connection with the Yucca Trail. The Yucca Trail will lead you back to West Boundary Road and the parking area. If that isn't enough for you in one day, you can always ride it again.

Don't be surprised if you find a trail that's not included in this guide. Central Arkansas Recreational Peddlers (CARP) members are continually building new trails in Camp Robinson.

A Central Arkansas Recreational Peddlers membership is required to ride at Camp Robinson. Members will receive a map of the trails and directions to Camp Robinson. Bring your driver's license, vehicle registration, and CARP card with you to the base entrance. If you don't have this information, you will not be allowed on base. Sign in at the Police Station before you head out to the trails. CARP memberships can be purchased at any bike shop in Little Rock or by logging on to www.carpclub.com and mailing in the membership application.

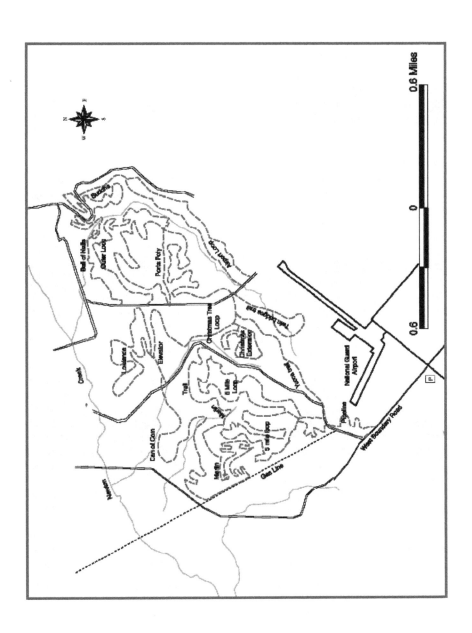

Allsopp Park Trail

19

Easy / Intermediate

Trail length: 5 miles
Ride time: Varies depending on length
Trail type: Singletrack; Stacked Loop System

directions

Allsopp Park is located in Little Rock, AR. From Interstate 40, take Interstate 430 south. Exit on Hwy. 10 east (Cantrell Rd.) and drive towards downtown Little Rock. Turn right on Cedar Hill Road. The park is on the right.

trail description

Allsopp Park is a great place to ride right in downtown Little Rock. The park is separated into two distinct areas: Allsopp Park North and Allsopp Park South. The south part of the park is located off of Cedar Hill Road. The trail can be accessed from the main parking area here or on Kavanaugh Boulevard on the south edge of the park. A 0.5-mile paved trail offers beginners a great place to ride. Starting from the parking lot, the best way to ride the trail is clockwise. Cross the street and climb up the section of trail that parallels Cedar Hill Road. At the top, cross a service road and follow the trail along the hillside. A spur trail will come in from the left that takes you to Kavanaugh Blvd. You'll descend to a stream crossing. Turn left before you cross the stream and follow the trail up the narrow valley. Follow the contour around the hollow. At the next intersection, the lower trail (right) will take you immediately back to the parking area. The upper trail, to the left, climbs back up and follows the contour along the hillside. There are two opportunities to take connecting trails that head straight downhill to the parking lot, or you can take Ash Street over to Allsopp Park North. If you head to Allsopp North, the trailhead is located near the intersection of South Lookout Road and Ash Street. Once you get to the trail, turn left at the intersection and ride the loop clockwise. You'll descend to a creek crossing and climb up the hill on the other side. Enjoy the descent all the way to Cantrell road. There are two trail options to ascend the valley. The trail along the stream starts as an access road and gradually narrows to singletrack. The south trail, to the left, parallels Allsopp Park road to the intersection with South Lookout Road. Take Ash Street back to Allsopp South

Hikers and other trail users enjoy the trails at Allsopp Park, so please be courteous to other trail users. This is not the best place to train for that next race, but it does offer riders a great getaway without having to drive out of town. Picnic tables and a pavilion are available for visitors. Water is available onsite. For more information, contact Little Rock Parks and Recreation at 501-571-6924.

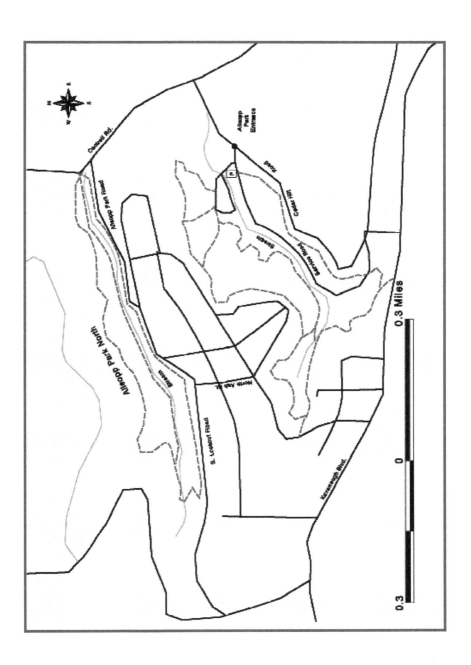

Boyle Park Trail
Easy / Intermediate

Trail length: 8 miles
Ride time: 20 minutes – 1 hour
Trail type: Singletrack and paved trail; Stacked Loop System

directions

Boyle Park is located in Little Rock, AR. From Interstate 40, take Interstate 430 south. Exit on Interstate 630 east. Drive to University Ave. (Hwy. 70) and turn right (south). Turn right on Cleveland Drive. When the road Y's, turn left on Boyle Park Road. The parking area will be on the right.

trail description

Boyle Park is another great place for mountain bikers to ride in Little Rock. The trails are not marked, so they may be a little difficult to find at first. Most of the trails are located on the northwest side of the park. There are two sections of trail located adjacent to Boyle Park Road. You can ride the entire trail system in an afternoon. The best place to park is on the east side of the park along Boyle Park Road. Starting at the parking area, take the paved bicycle path to the right. Before crossing the bridge on the left, turn right and cross Boyle Park Road. Then ride past the park sign and climb up the hill to the left. This section of singletrack climbs and descends several times before popping out on Archwood Drive. Turn right on Archwood Drive and turn left on to Boyle Park Road. Look for the trail on the right side of the road. Follow the benchcut trail along the hillside and then descend down to the old road through the park, which is closed to traffic. Follow the paved road back to the parking lot or turn left, cross the bridge, and continue to ride the rest of the trail on the northwest part of the park. An access road to the left is barricaded. The trail crosses the road just past the barricades. Turn right and climb up a steep section of trail. Cross the road and turn right onto the singletrack. There are several loop options in this area. Stay to the right at the trail intersections and ride the outer loop or use some of the connecting trails. You'll have to explore this area to get used to the trail. As you make your way to the backside of the park, descend down to a small creek. Do not turn right at the bottom. This trail dead ends at an apartment complex (the map does not show this trail on purpose). Follow the creek downstream, crossing the first paved road to the road crossing with the barricades mentioned earlier. Ride a loop around the park on the paved bicycle trail or head straight to the main parking area.

There are picnic tables and a pavilion available to visitors. Restrooms and water are available onsite. Bring your fishing pole and try your luck at the pond. Don't forget your fishing license. Boyle Park is a great place for the whole family. For more information, contact Little Rock Parks and Recreation at 501-571-6924.

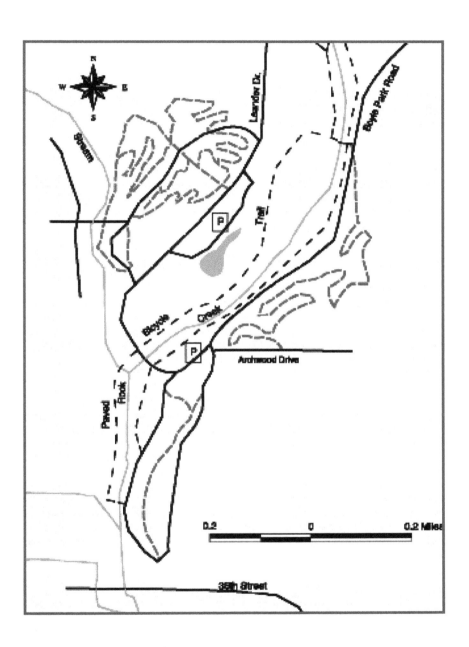

Section 13 Trail

Intermediate

Trail length: 10 miles
Ride time: 45 minutes – 2 hours
Trail type: Singletrack and dirt roads; Stacked Loop System

directions

Section 13 is located west of Little Rock, AR. From Interstate 430 in Little Rock, drive west on Hwy. 10 (Cantrell Road) approximately 8.5 miles. Turn left (south) on Garrison Road. Drive about 2.2 miles. The trailhead will be on the left side of the road. Park anywhere in the gravel parking lot.

trail description

Section 13 Trails are made up of a combination of singletrack and dirt road trails on a 640-acre tract of land. Local mountain bikers have taken the responsibility of building a trail system within this area. The trail is marked with temporary maps of the trail system at most of the intersections. Head south out of the parking lot and turn right onto the singletrack located just past the gate. You'll immediately climb a series of tight turns over rocky terrain and narrow drainages. The trail splits half way up. The trail to the left takes more experienced riders through a lot of exposed rocks. Stay to the right for a little easier section of trail. When you reach the top of the climb, cross an unimproved 4-wheeler trail. The trail descends on the other side through a set of switchbacks and crosses a dirt road. You can bail out here by turning left and following the dirt road back to the trailhead. Continue on the other side of the road. The trail climbs and descends several times through a series of steep switchbacks. Keep your bike under control through this area. The line of sight is limited. You'll eventually come out onto a dirt road on the southeast corner of the park. Turn left and climb uphill to the first road intersection. Follow the ridge to the west for a while before descending back to the trailhead. Be careful. The road is washed out in several sections. There will be options to ride dirt road loops to the north (first turn to the right) and the south (left at the second intersection) as you ride along the ridge if you want to get more miles in.

Mountain bikers from Little Rock are building more trails all the time, so don't be surprised to find a new section of trail on your next visit to Section 13. There are no restrooms or water available onsite, so you will need to come prepared. Stock up at one of the convenience stores/gas stations located along Hwy. 10 as you leave Little Rock. For more information, contact Little Rock Parks and Recreation at 501-571-6924.

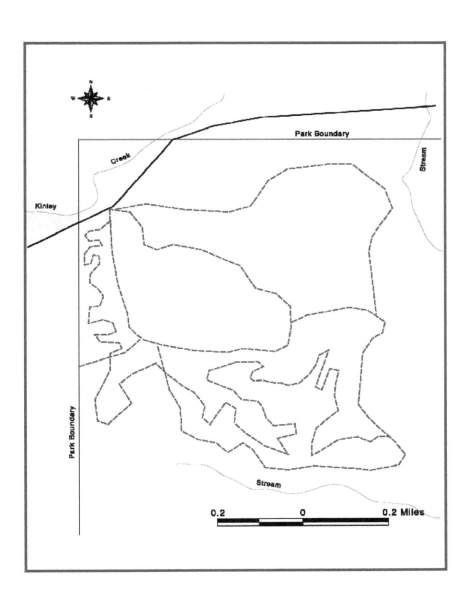

Park Boundary

Creek

Kinley

Stream

Park Boundary

Stream

0.2   0   0.2 Miles

National and Local Mountain Bike Groups

International Mountain Bike Association
P.O. Box 7578
Boulder, CO 80306
Jenn Dice; 303-545-9011
www.imba.com

Ozark Off Road Cyclists
Phi Penny; 479-445-8212
www.ozarkoffroadcyclists.com

Twin Lakes Bicycle Club
123 CR 1159
Gassville, AR 72635
Jim Holsted; 870-425-9400
www.norfork.com/cycling

Batesville Independent Knobby Explorers
2121 Harrison Street
Batesville, AR 72501
Rick Sederberg; 870-793-7370
rockdoc@indco.net

Central Arkansas Recreational Peddlers
6004 Buffalo River Road
N. Little Rock, AR 72116
Gary Lamb; 501-835-6721
www.carpclub.com

Hot Springs Bicycle Association
P.O. Box 20874
Hot Springs, AR 71901
Gary Strakshus
www.bikearkansas.com/hsba

Bike Shop List

Northwest Arkansas

Champion Cycling
and Fitness
1702 S. Walton Blvd.
Bentonville, AR
(479) 464-9500

Highroller Cyclery Inc.
322 W. Spring
Fayetteville, AR
(479) 442-9311

Lewis & Clark Outfitters
4915 S. Thompson
Springdale, AR
(479) 756-1344

Ozark Bike Shop Inc.
400 Hwy 71
Rogers, AR
(479) 636-0394

North Central Arkansas

Bikes and Things inc.
223 Russell Ln.
Mountain Home, AR
(870) 424-4642

Bicycle Outfitters of Bryant
605 N. Reynolds Rd.
Bryant, AR
(501) 847-3200

Western Arkansas

Bicycles Etc.
1500 Grand Ave.
Fort Smith, AR
(479) 783-4981

Bicycles of Fort Smith
7613 Rogers Ave.
Fort Smith, AR
(479) 478-7500

Champion Cycling & Fitness
8824 Rogers Ave
Fort Smith, AR
(479) 484-7500

Carr's Chain Reaction Bicycle
201 W. Parkway Dr. #D
Russelleville, AR
(479) 890-4950

Highlander Cycling
& Outdoors
1001 N. Arkansas Ave.
Russelleville, AR
(479) 967-4699

Poppa Wheelies
316 West B Str.
Russelleville, AR
(479) 890-6665

Central Arkansas

Arkansas Cycling and Fitness
3010 E. Kiehl Ave
Little Rock, AR
(501) 834-5787

Arkansas Cycling & Fitness #2
400 N. Bowman Curve Rd.
Suite 32
Little Rock, AR
(501) 221-BIKE

Bike City
2212 W. Beebe Capps Express
Searcy, AR
(501)278-5515

Bikeseller.com
2222 Cantrell Rd.
Little Rock, AR
(501) 663-8796

Chainwheel
10300 Rodney Parham Rd.
Little Rock, AR
(501) 224-7651

J & P Bike Shop
7910 Highway 107
Sherwood, AR
(501) 835-4814

The Ride
2100 Meadow Lake, Ste. 2
Conway, AR
(501) 764-4500

Southwest Bike Shop
7121 Baseline Rd.
Little Rock, AR
(501)562-1866

Land Manager Contact Information

U.S. Forest Service

Bayou Ranger District
12000 SR 27
Hector, AR 72843
Phone: 479-284-3150

Boston Mountain
Ranger District
P.O. Box 76
Hwy. 23 North
Ozark, AR 72949
Phone: 479-667-2191

Buffalo Ranger District
P.O. Box 427
Hwy. 7 North
Jasper, AR 72641
Phone: 870-446-5122

Cass Job Corps Center
HC 63, Box 219
Ozark, AR 72949
Phone: 479-667-3686

Magazine Ranger District
P.O. Box 511
Hwy. 22 E & Kalamazo
Paris, AR 72855
Phone: 479-963-3076

Pleasant Hill
Ranger District
P.O. Box 190
Hwy. 21 North
Clarksville, AR 72830
Phone: 479-754-2864

St. Francis Ranger District
2675 Hwy. 44
Marianna, AR 72360
Phone: 870-295-5278

Sylamore Ranger District
609 Sylamore Ave.
Mtn. View, AR 72560
Phone: 870-269-3228

National Park Service

Buffalo National River
P.O. Box 1173
Harrison, AR 72602
Phone: 870-741-5443

Arkansas State Parks

Arkansas State
Trails Coordinator
One Capitol Mall
Little Rock, AR 72201
Phone: 501-682-1301

Devil's Den State Park
11333 West Hwy. 74
West Fork, AR 72774
Phone: 479-761-3325

Hobbs State Park
– Conservation Area
20344 East Hwy. 12
Rogers, AR 72756
Phone: 479-789-2380

Ozark Folk Center
State Park
P.O. Box 500
Mountain View, AR 72560
Phone: 870-269-3851

Mount Magazine
State Park
16878 Hwy. 309 South
Paris, AR 72855
Phone: 479-963-8502

Mt. Nebo State Park
#1 State Park Drive
Dardanelle, AR 72834
Phone: 479-229-3655

U.S. Army Corps of
Engineers

Beaver Lake Office
2260 N. 2nd Street
Rogers, AR 72756-2439
Phone: (479) 636-1210

Lake Dardanelle
Field Office
1598 Lock and Dam Road
Russelleville, AR 72801
(479) 968-5008

Mountain Home
Project Office
324 W. 7th Street
Mountain Home, AR
72653
(870) 425-2700

Ozark Field Office
6042 Lock and Dam Road
Ozark, AR 72949-2129
(479) 667-2129

If you're interested in finding out more about trails in Arkansas, log on to www.bikearkansas.com. This website is an excellent source of information about cycling clubs, bike shops, lodging, trails, public lands, advocacy, etc.

CPSIA information can be obtained
at www.ICGtesting.com
Printed in the USA
LVHW040043091218
599781LV00034BA/1385/P